*Sas*  ...*sents*...

# 20 RULES FOR INVESTING SUCCESS

### Mental Insights to Trading and Investing on the Stock Market

Copyright © 2019 Sasha Evdakov

All rights reserved.

Version 2.02

| | |
|---|---|
| COPYRIGHT NOTICE | 4 |
| QUICK RESOURCES | 5 |
| TRADING DISCLAIMER | 6 |
| INTRODUCTION | 8 |
| RULE #1 | 10 |
| RULE #2 | 12 |
| RULE #3 | 14 |
| RULE #4 | 16 |
| RULE #5 | 19 |
| RULE #6 | 21 |
| RULE #7 | 23 |
| RULE #8 | 25 |
| RULE #9 | 27 |
| RULE #10 | 29 |
| RULE #11 | 32 |
| RULE #12 | 34 |
| RULE #13 | 37 |
| RULE #14 | 39 |
| RULE #15 | 42 |
| RULE #16 | 44 |
| RULE #17 | 46 |
| RULE #18 | 48 |
| RULE #19 | 50 |
| RULE #20 | 52 |
| FINAL THANK YOU & RESOURCES | 54 |

# COPYRIGHT NOTICE

I love spreading knowledge in the world, educating other people, and helping others achieve their potential. You are welcome to cite things from this book; however, please give credit back to me or my website https://tradersfly.com, https://rise2learn.com, or https://sashaevdakov.com

If you have any questions regarding the copyright or would like to use parts of it on your website, presentation, contact me from my stock trading website https://tradersfly.com or my personal website https://sashaevdakov.com

## COPYRIGHT FROM THE LAWYERS

Please do **not** distribute, copy, or create derivate works of this book as it contains material protected under International and Federal Copyright Laws and Treaties. Any unauthorized reprint or use of this material is prohibited. No part of this book may be reproduced or transmitted in any form or by any means, electronic or mechanical, including photocopying, recording, or by any information storage and retrieval system without express written permission from the author / publisher.

Okay, enough with that. Let's get into it!

# QUICK RESOURCES

Before you get too far, I want to give you a handful of resources that may be of help.

- https://tradersfly.com: Free stock trading educational lessons on video
- https://members.tradersfly.com: All of our stock trading membership plans where we have premium content, group coaching, and market insight
- https://rise2learn.com: All of our course listings, classes, and other books where you can get detailed training and live webinars
- https://backstageincome.com: Online business website that can help you jumpstart an online business and grow your online presence
- https://sashaevdakov.com: My personal website which will showcase my current projects

With that being said… let's get rolling!

# TRADING DISCLAIMER

Sasha Evdakov or Rise2Learn, LLC are not licensed, financial advisers. Nothing contained in our material is intended to be or construed to be as financial advice. All information on any media is not intended as investment, tax, accounting, or legal advice. Nor is it an offer, endorsement, or recommendation to buy, sell, or trade any company, security, or fund.

To read our full disclaimer, please visit https://rise2learn.com

## INVOLVES RISK AND IS NOT SUITABLE FOR ALL INVESTORS

Online trading has inherent risk due to system response and access times that may vary due to market conditions, system performance, and other factors. An investor should understand these and additional risks before trading.

Content, research, tools, and stock or option symbols are for entertainment, educational, and illustrative purposes only and do not imply a recommendation or solicitation to buy or sell a particular security or to engage in any specific investment strategy. The projections or other information regarding the likelihood of various investment outcomes are hypothetical and are not guarantees of future results.

You agree that all content, including all media under Rise2Learn, LLC along with its materials, are proprietary rights and that their use is restricted by the terms of this agreement. Use of the content, media, or material, for any purpose without written permission from Rise2Learn, LLC is strictly prohibited. You further agree that you will not create derivate works of this media, material, or products offered by Rise2Learn, LLC.

Rise2Learn does not guarantee or promise any income or particular result from your use of the information contained herein. Rise2Learn, LLC assumes no responsibility or liability for issues, errors, or omissions in the information in our media.

To read our full trading disclaimer, please visit https://rise2learn.com

## DAMAGES AND LIABILITIES

Rise2Learn will not be liable for any incidental, indirect, direct, punitive, consequential, special, exemplary, or other damages including, but not limited to, loss of revenue or income, pain, and suffering, emotional distress, or similar damages even if Rise2Learn has been advised of the possibility of such damages.

In no event will the collective liability to any party (regardless of the form of action, whether in contract, tort, or otherwise) exceed greater of $100 or the amount you have paid to Rise2Learn for the information product, service, seminar, or media out of which liability arose. Under no circumstances will Rise2Learn be liable for any loss or damage caused by your reliance on the information contained herein.

It is your responsibility to evaluate the accuracy, completeness, or usefulness of any information, advice, opinion, or other content contained in any media presented by Rise2Learn. Please seek the advice of professionals, as appropriate, regarding the evaluation of any specific information, advice, opinion, or content, or media.

To read our full trading disclaimer, please visit https://rise2learn.com

# Introduction

Thank you for joining me in this book!

Some of the rules that I mentioned throughout this book I have mentioned dozens of times on my YouTube channel and discussed the concepts in my other books like the 100 Stock Trading Tips.

My goal in writing this book was to give you a simplified version of some common rules that you should think about before investing or trading stocks.

You may or may not agree with all of these rules. I understand that you will probably have a different trading style, system, strategy, risk tolerance, and other factors that are unique to you. However, I wanted to bring some of these concepts to your attention so that at least you understand the principles in my mind when it comes to trading so that at the minimum you could keep them in the back of your mind.

At the bare minimum, if you are aware of these concepts, it will allow you to craft a system and strategy that is right for you even if you only use bits and pieces of a specific concept.

While going through this book, remember to keep an open mind. First, go through the book and be open to all the rules mentioned in this book. This will allow you to embrace the concepts truly. Then later, you can fine-tune some of these concepts to make them your own. In the end, it's all about finding your system, your strategy, and doing what works for you.

Use this book to your advantage to help you move in the right direction, improve your trading, and ultimately allow you to improve your life as you create success for yourself.

Let's get started!

# Rule #1

# No one will care about your money more than you!

One of the things that I truly believe is that **no one will care more about your money than you!** Unless of course, you simply don't care about your money...

Even if you have a personal financial advisor that understands your financial situation, they still don't live inside your brain, feel what you feel, or get the true insight behind your deepest thoughts, your goals, or vision.

Handing your money over to a mutual fund or a professional investor is a choice that many people may go with – however, remember that the person on the other end cares first about themselves. Then they care about their job. Then they may care about you, and after that, if you are lucky, they may care about your money.

You might be thinking: **"but it's their job to grow your money..."**

Think of it this way: how many people do you know that truly love their job every single day when they walk into work? Have you always loved your job? Have you ever moved on to do something different or have you done the same thing for the last 10, 20, or 30 years?

**These money managers are no different!**

They will invest your money, and they will take care of it until they get a better job offering, get fired, or have kids, and then you will get pushed to another person.

If it's a major mutual fund company that actively invests your money, then they may stick your money into a basic index fund similar to the SPY, QQQ, or IWM or they may purchase 2-5 stocks. Then each month they will send you a report, but these monthly reports are a decorative veneer as before the end of the month they reshuffle positions to show you "favorable stocks." Stocks that look better on paper.

But are they going to check your positions day to day? Probably not...

**Will they care if you lose a bunch of money?** Probably not...

They might care if you decide to leave them as a customer as it affects their business – but they wouldn't care that you made only $700 this year on your $50,000 versus the other guy who made $10,000.

In the end, **the person who will care most about your money is YOU!**

# Rule #2

## Keep your portfolio clean!

Have you ever walked into someone's home, and it was a messy disaster? Have you ever tried to look for your keys or wallet, but had a hard time finding them?

That's what clutter does to us – it displaces our focus, we don't run efficiently, and it costs us time and energy.

A messy house may cost you time and energy to clean it, but **a messy portfolio will cost you hard-earned money!**

First, **what is a messy portfolio?**

A messy portfolio is a group of investments where you cannot quickly evaluate the investments. **It is a portfolio that wastes your time.**

**Having a messy portfolio is like trying to chase a horse through an obstacle course.** There is no way you are going to catch that horse! You are going to stumble over the jumps, fall in the mud, and get winded.

This is **extremely dangerous** when you trade stocks. If you can't find what you need, if you can't quickly evaluate what you need to do – your account is going to suffer!

You might be wondering how do you keep a clean portfolio? **You keep things simple!**

One of the problems I constantly see with new traders is they want to "WATCH OR FIND MORE STOCKS" or "TRADE MORE STOCKS." – **These are huge mistakes!**

**A little piece of advice:** if you have less than a $1,000,000 account you should be trading less than five stocks! – **That's right... five stocks MAX!**

Trading less stocks will allow you to focus on those key stocks. I know that many investors will tell you to be diversified, and having a group of five stocks is great, but there is more management that goes along with trading more stocks.

Speaking about your watch list... why do you need 50 stocks in your watch list? Or 100 stocks in your watch list? **Focus on the best companies** – the ones that will move the fastest in the shortest amount of time!

**Cut the clutter in your watch list, cut the clutter in your positions, and clean up your watch list and portfolio so that you can manage positions efficiently!**

# Rule #3

# Keep things simple! You don't have to be an investor guru

Trying to become a professional sports player in every sport is a recipe for **failure**! Remember when Michael Jordan tried to play golf and baseball? It didn't work out very well...

Mixing professions is exceptionally difficult! For this reason, it is rare for you to see a professional hockey player who also is a professional tennis player. Even within hockey, you have specialists – you don't see a goalie playing center. **A goalie focuses on what he knows best – protecting the goal.**

**How do these professionals make their millions? They stick to their focus**, their core, their specialty, and their **single professional position doing the same thing consistently.**

When it comes to trading, there are many roads you can take. You can trade Forex, stocks, options, commodities, bonds, and many other things. Within these, there are even sub-categories. Under stock trading, you have blue-chip, penny stocks, recent IPOs, etc. Within options, you have strategies like calendars, verticals, iron condors, butterflies, etc.

With all these opportunities, **what should an investor do?** Do you need to trade everything? Do you need to know everything under the sun about car repair and mechanics to fix a flat tire? – **NO!** You need to know how to lift the car and change a tire. You don't have to know how the engine works.

You don't have to be a guru at every single thing in trading!

**You need to learn a single simple strategy that works for you consistently** to where every time you see a situation or opportunity, you can place a trade and make money.

You need to find that single method and strategy in investing that works for you!

**First, choose your main sport when it comes to investing.** Is it going to be stocks, bonds, ETFs, commodities, options, or something else?

**Then choose your position within that sport.** If you picked stocks – what kind of stocks are you going to invest in? Blue-chip? Small-cap? Penny stocks? If you picked options, then what vehicles, stocks, or ETFs are you going to trade? What will be your strategy? Are you going to do calendars, butterflies, iron condors, or a mix?

In the end, **you have to keep things simple...** You don't have to know everything. **You simply have to find what works FOR YOU!**

# Rule #4

## Don't buy everything at once

It is rare to buy a stock at the bottom and sell it at the top. It does happen, but it is not something you will be able to do consistently. Not to mention, are you looking for a bottom and top within the daily action? The weekly chart, monthly chart, or in the lifetime of the stock? Everyone's timeframe is different!

Similar to how you should never use all of your account capital to buy one stock (because you need room to make adjustments if things go against you) – you should **not** buy your full position at one time.

Remember that stocks pull back, they retrace, power higher, and then **they may have counter-trend bounces that suck you in!**

How do you know if you are in a counter-trend bounce or a segment that should power higher? **It is difficult.**

After studying the markets for years, I have a good grasp when this happens, but even I cannot predict this with 100% certainty…

And if I'm not certain, then I need to take caution on the risks involved which is **why I do not jump in head-first with all my capital at once.**

Buy it in quarters if you have a large account. You can buy it in thirds or halves if you have a smaller account. This allows you to put less risk on the table initially and **if the stock goes against you completely – you are out!** (And you didn't take as large of a hit as you would have.)

Of course, if it went higher you would not make as much – but again I can't stress this enough… **this business is about risk and money management!** Not about profit daydreaming.

**Let the stock prove to you that it is moving higher** from your buy point and then you can buy more at a higher price – at least in this case it proved to you that it was worth the investment!

**Why don't more people use the scaling strategy?**

There are probably a few reasons behind this. They might want the quick and fast money (meaning they are looking at their potential profits)… or they might not have a large account, and they are trying to save on commissions…

When you have this mentality – **it is a dangerous mentality!**

Think about it for a second – **you are trying to save $7 in trade commissions when you could be risking thousands of dollars!**

**That logic doesn't make sense…**

Focus on the risk that you are putting on the table and buy in stages.

If you want a 1,000 share position buy 300 shares first, then maybe another 300 shares, and then your final 400 shares. **You don't have to get in all at once.**

What's the difference if you spread your risk out over multiple days or weeks, especially if you plan to hold a stock for multiple weeks, months, or even years?

Think about it.

# Rule #5

## Always take profits into strength

Just like you should not buy your full position at once, you shouldn't sell your full position at one time.

I always tell my coaching students to **take a quarter, a third, or half off into strength as the stock moves in your favor!**

**This business is about taking money off the table!**

Since you can't perfectly time the top or the bottom you need to take your money off the table – or else the market will take your money when you start selling in a panic.

**Why does this happen?**

It's simple – when things are moving in your favor, you feel good and content. You want more money and greed kicks in. This leads you to holding your position.

Once things start to turn around, people start taking their profits, and the selling accelerates – **that exit door is never big enough!**

Have you ever seen those Black Friday shoppers after Thanksgiving on TV that camp outside the store? Then when the doors open how people rush through that one single door?

It's an animal house! **That door is never big enough** to allow that many people through at once!

This is what happens in the stock market... once the selling starts, panic and fear kick in, which overtakes your greedy state earlier because **fear is a stronger emotion!**

It forces you to sell your stock just like all the other people.

The difference is – **were you the smart one who took half your profits at the higher prices when things were good? Or were you the greedy Bozo that wanted more?**

In the end, always take some profits into strength to reduce your risk!

It will give you peace of mind that if and when that stock comes back, you can get out at your entry point and you would still be profitable.... because you were the smart one who took half of your profits off into strength!

**Get into the habit of taking profits into strength!**

# Rule #6

## Don't worry about taxes & profits – focus on risk!

I hate paying taxes – probably like you do!

I would love to pay higher taxes if I felt like I got a return on my money and the government managed the financial system like I manage my bank accounts – but they don't, and we have major debt on our books similar to how most people have credit card debt.

This is not the way I live or manage my accounts, but this is how the majority of people live, and the government will continue to blow my hard-earned money! These things are out of my control so why waste mental energy focusing on it?

**What is the right thing to focus on?** Risk... and money management and then, of course, making more money.

You see if you focus on cutting your taxes, saving money, and pinching pennies, there is only so much you can save.

**However, your profits are unlimited!**

In addition, if you constantly focus on saving more then **your subconscious mentality may play a trick on you that you should make less so that you can pay less taxes – this is a terrible mentality to have.**

Instead, I prefer to reframe this tax issue that we all deal with. Here is what I say to myself...

"I WANT TO PAY A LOT OF TAXES. I WANT A BIGGER TAX BILL THIS YEAR THAN LAST YEAR!"

Why would I say something like this? Because I know that if I get a bigger tax bill at the end of the year, my earnings will be much greater. It is a cause and effect relationship since the taxes are out of my control.

Remember that a high-income tax problem is a good problem to have.

# Rule #7

# Stop following people blindly – have your own system & strategy

If you are new to investing you still might be trying to find your style, methods, and see what works for you!

You know a mini-van is not the ideal vehicle for everyone... Some people love convertibles, and other people love trucks. Alligators love the swamp, and the polar bears love the Arctic Circle.

But you can't be an alligator following the polar bear's footsteps in the Arctic Circle!

This is exactly what people do when it comes to investing. **They follow people they shouldn't!**

They think that the other person knows more. Maybe because they are on Stocktwits, Twitter, YouTube, Facebook, or on TV.

**Remember that the person on TV or some social media is NOT you!**

They don't know your goals, risk tolerance, trading preference, experience, or trading account size!

Everyone will have a different reason for putting on a trade. They may have a different long term plan. They have a larger account than you. There are a lot of variables, and even if you follow someone in a chat room, **there is always going to be a lag time.**

**Everyone is unique** and has a one of a kind investing profile that fits them. You may be able to find someone you can relate to that takes you to the next level, pushes you to learn more, or gives you ideas and concepts – but **in the end, your final trading strategy and system are going to be something that you personally create.**

You may get ideas from various sources, but ultimately it is you who is going to tweak it to your liking and make it your own.

**Stop following everyone blindly.**

If you follow someone, understand why they choose the stocks that they do. Why they put on a certain trade and not another. Don't follow too many people because it will only confuse you.

**Follow a select few people that you can relate to that make YOU better and whose ideas help you create your strategy and system.**

# Rule #8

## TV is for entertainment – stop investing in what they say

Do you love to watch TV shows or movies? Have you seen *Iron Man, Superman,* or any of the *Batman* films?

Yeah, me too! They were **great entertainment....**

Do I invest in Halloween costumes, tech gadgets, or the movie studios because I saw an entertaining movie?

**Absolutely NOT!**

Television, movies, and shows are there for entertainment purposes ONLY!

**If you are watching TV for investment advice – you will get burnt.**

Remember that the goal of TV stations is to have a higher viewership. How do you get a higher viewership? You **report fear, emotional topics, and things that catch attention.**

Why do you think the 6:00 or 9:00 news stories mostly feature drugs, shootings, fires, and other major topics? It is because if they showed you the kid who helped an elderly neighbor cut her grass, they wouldn't get the same viewership.

**The television is there for entertainment purposes. It isn't there to advise you what to buy or what to sell.**

And those analysts on TV... many of them have a bigger agenda.

**When they tell you to buy a stock, they are looking to get out of it** – because they are already in the stock.

**When they tell you to sell the stock, they are looking to get in it at lower prices** because they missed the move.

**Quit buying into the hype of the television for your investments!**

The television is there for your entertainment – not for you to make investment decisions.

# Rule #9

# Hope and prayer are for religion – not investing

Hope and prayer is a good thing when it comes to religion.

Churches bring together communities who help one another. Hope and prayer help those who need that shining light in the distance. These are all great things in society, but **these are terrible things for investing!**

When you "hope" for something, you are tying emotion to it, and **this business will kill you if you trade or invest based on emotions!**

I find that many investors who get stuck in positions (you know when they loaded up on a stock in the high $90 per share price and now the stock is $20 bucks) – they hope and pray for it to come back.

Initially, when that stock was selling off, they prayed that it would come back to their breakeven point.

Then that loss became bigger. It turned into a $5,000 loss, $30,000 loss, and a $80,000 loss! Then they hoped that it would come back just a bit, so their loss is only $30,000 instead of $80,000!

**This is why you don't want to invest based on hope!**

**You will get stuck into positions for years!**

Over the years, I've spoken to people who have been holding stocks for more than 10 years because they bought at the highs and now are stuck in that position.

Now that stock is a few bucks and it's struggling to break out of that price range, and they can't sell it because of their "hope" or fear of missing out at getting out at breakeven.

If you find yourself in this situation – **GET OUT!**

**Sell your position and move on.**

Learn the word "next" in this business because you can take that remaining cash and put it into a better position that grows your account instead of "hoping" or "praying" that it comes back.

Most of the time, once a stock gets into those cheap levels, it takes years for it to get out of that dog house.

# Rule #10

## Get the best stocks – not the cheapest

When you shop at a store, society has programmed us to look for a few different things such as the best deal, the greatest bargain, the highest quality, and the cheapest price.

One of the natural mindsets we humans have been programmed with is for us to maximize the value we get. Many times this means looking for the best bargain or the cheapest price.

Due to this mental programming, it's no wonder that **many investors look for the cheapest priced stocks**. They believe that by buying a stock at a low price it is unlikely for the stock to go much lower... and that you are getting a bargain buy.

After all, a stock can only go down to zero.

However, an expensive stock may already be overextended. It may be over-priced and not have much room left to run.

So what do most people do? **They go for cheap stocks!** But **this is a horrible investment mindset!** Unfortunately, it is one mentality we are programmed with that works against us when it comes to investments.

The main advantage you have when it comes to shopping at the store is that you are familiar with the brands and the products. You can typically spot which products taste great, feel great, work well, and do what you need them to do because you have experience with them or with similar products.

With company investments, more than likely, you don't go and interview their management team. You don't go and review their accounting books. You can't do that, and many other things are beneath the surface. You don't have the experience of spotting certain things because you haven't been trading and investing as long as you have been buying groceries.

Think about your level of understanding when you go to make that investment. Focus on quality because you want an investment to last... like you would want a durable product such as a washing machine to last. You don't want a cheap washing machine that breaks in six months.

Now it's time for the big test. **Why are certain products at the store more expensive than others?** More than likely, because the quality is not the same as the cheaper products.

In business, you will pay a higher price for things that have more value, such as better service, outstanding delivery, great quality, and the marketing of the product. That means when you see cheaper products, remember that **they are usually cheap for a reason!**

The same is true when you are putting your money on the line with your investments. **If you think that cheap stocks have a higher potential to go up... think again.**

**Which stocks are the ones that come to your mind right away as being the best investments?** Probably stocks like Amazon, Facebook, Apple, Netflix, Tesla, etc.

Can these stocks go bust eventually? **Absolutely!** Do they always have an uptrend? **No, they don't!** They are the ones that in general have been moving up over the last few years. **They have a track history of moving higher.**

Compare that to a cheapo stock XYZ. That cheap stock is typically traded by the day traders or penny stock traders. This is NOT where the billionaire investors are putting their money.

**Follow the money. Stick to the best investments that have a track history. Not the ones that are "cheap."**

If you focus on "cheap" stocks, eventually you will get a serious breakdown because they are, after all – cheap for a reason.

# Rule #11

# The key is knowing what to do when you get in trouble

One of the key things that I learned in this business is that "**you have to learn what to do when you get into trouble.**"

Anyone can slap on a few trades and when those trades keep going up every single day – it's easy!

**The real test is what you will do when your positions start to go against you!**

That is what is going to separate a temporary investor from someone who's going to be in this business a long time.

Most people think their position will be fine, but this is the trick that your mind will play on you...

Maybe because you say to yourself "I've done my homework" or "this stock continues to move higher – just look at that chart" or for some other reason. These are all great things to convince yourself of the future – but **what is your risk management plan? What if it doesn't work out that way? What will you do?**

**Everything does NOT work 100% of the time.**

We all expect to win our sports games – but sometimes we lose.

We all expect to be kind, but sometimes we are hateful.

We all expect to be on time for dinner, but sometimes we are late.

Having some plan for when things go against you (even if it's a bad plan) is better than no plan at all – because when crap hits the fan, you need to take care of the mess...

**Otherwise, you are going to lose a great deal of money!**

**Knowing what to do in this business is critical to your success.**

# Rule #12

# Be realistic - you don't live in Disney World

We all dream of our stocks exploding to the upside... and we all want it to move immediately after we buy that stock, but things don't work like that in the stock market...

It's **at Disney World where your dreams are a reality.**

When you visit a Disney park, there are magical things that happen. You get to see the prince, princesses, magical creatures, and experience a world that you've never seen before. When you see that world, it feels great, exciting, and you get that warm fuzzy feeling.

Then when you leave the park and you get to your car, you turn the key, and the car doesn't start. Great – a dead battery, three hungry kids, and no jumper cables! Welcome back to the real world.

Be realistic – **you can't live in la-la-land forever, but that is exactly what people do in the markets!**

I find that many people who start trading on the stock market **"believe"** in their stock, they **imagine it** (and **dream about it**) will power higher. And **if it only gets up to $120 per share** they can buy their dream house.

When you look at that stock, it's a $4-dollar stock that has been less than $5 for the last 10 years! **Come on – be real.**

A $4 stock "can" turn into a $120 stock, **but is it likely? – not really**... with time... maybe, but not probable.

The same thing is true if you are looking at stock trends. **Don't get sucked into the hype that stocks will go up every single day.**

Remember that stocks consolidate and go through an accumulation period and then they power higher. After which they may pull back (retracement) or move sideways. Then again, you may see another move to the upside for a brief period.

**You are not going to get a stock to uptick every single day! That isn't real!** Nor is it healthy for that stock.

When it comes to daily moves if you see a $5 stock that typically moves 20 cents a day and **today it is powering higher by $3... take some profits!** It is over-extended.

If you see a $95 stock that normally moves $2 to $5 per day and now it's moving higher by $25 in a single day – **again take some profits off the table!**

Remember that **the market is like a rubber band.** It comes back to the average price point due to being overextended in one direction or another. This is why you need sideways moves which gives a stock time to digest.

**You can't have higher prices every single day!**

You need to be **realistic about the movements...**

A rocket ship to the moon is great for space travel, but eventually, it comes back down, and sometimes you get catastrophic explosions.

**When you see a stock moving higher in a straight line like a rocket ship – take some profits off whether it is half, a third, or a quarter because eventually that stock is going to pull back.**

Be realistic about the movements, probabilities, and potential – don't live in Disney World when it comes to your investments!

# Rule #13

## Think like a contrarian because most investors are wrong!

Most investors are wrong, and 90% of investors lose money!

In fact, **most fail completely within five years** and blow up their account significantly to the point that they don't trade anymore.

WHY IS THIS AND HOW DOES THIS HAPPEN?

It happens for a few different reasons. One of those reasons is our natural human programming. **We are not wired to think differently**, be different, and go against our natural human programming.

Even though you may think that you are an individual and have your unique thoughts, you still follow the rules of society, there are celebrities you probably look up to, and **your decisions are based on society's unintentional programming on you over the years.**

Here is what happens with a general investor...

Stocks have a major sell-off and then slowly start to climb back up over a year. The general investor then starts to "think" and "talk" about investing with his friends about the market as the market continues to climb higher now for its second year.

By the time we get to the end of year two, the general investor puts in his money. Over the next year, the market moves sideways having little pops from time to time. We start getting into distribution territory for the market, but **the general investor is unaware of this.**

A year later, the market has a major turn and continues to move lower **wiping out the general investor and causing him to sell his investments in a panic.**

**You see the general investor typically will buy at the highs and sell at the lows.** This is why most retail investors lose money. **They are always too early or too late.** They think and follow the "herd" and do exactly what everyone is telling them to do.

The general investor doesn't have a plan, a strategy, nor does he think on his own – this is what eventually leads to their demise.

Regarding this rule, one of the things I tell my coaching students is to "SELL WHEN THEY ARE SCREAMING TO BUY, AND BUY WHEN THEY ARE SCREAMING TO SELL."

Nevertheless, start thinking differently... **think on your own - quit following the herd.** Otherwise, you will get the same results as everyone else... putting you in the 90% failure rate.

# Rule #14

## Management is a big part of this business – learn to manage well

Management is a key component to investing and trading stocks. It fits along with the same principle as having a great leader or manager in a business. You want someone who can show you the vision and the direction that a business should move toward.

**With poor management or leadership, a business is doomed.**

Within your investment business, your goal is to manage your investments to the best of your ability so that at the end of your time, your business is profitable.

**Remember that your investment business... is your business! You are in the business of buying and selling a stock.**

You buy a stock at a lower price and sell it for a higher price similar to how a cell phone manufacturer buys parts at a lower price, puts it together, and sells it at a higher price.

When you look at your investment business, you need to learn how to manage it properly.

**You have to figure out what inventory is going bad and get rid of it** – or what's selling or producing your income and get more of it!

If you compare this to owning a fruit & vegetable stand business, you know that between apples, bananas, carrots, and potatoes some produce is going to rot faster than others.

Typically, the bananas will spoil first. This means it is important for you to get rid of it. **It would be best if you can sell them so you can make some money.**

**How does this apply to stocks?**

If you see a stock tanking, sick, or acting weak – you might want to get rid of it. Why are you going to hang on to something that is spoiling? **You don't have to wait around for the fruit flies... just get rid of it.**

On the other hand, if in your fruit & vegetable business you have your carrots selling like hotcakes and you constantly run out of supply – it would be wise to get more of them since they have a longer shelf life.

Similarly, if you have a stock that is bringing you consistent income then you should own a larger chunk of it. It has proven to you that this stock is worth the money and investment.

You can see how large of role management plays in the stock market.

Although, it may be easier to see this from a fruit & vegetable business because you are familiar with the products as you've been eating them for years.

With the stock market, it may be more difficult since you might not be as familiar with the companies, stock movements, and how things behave in the market... but you will get there.

It takes time, but you will get there.

Learn to manage your investments properly because you don't want to hold on to spoiled inventory – the longer you hold it, the worse and smellier it gets.

# Rule #15

# Extreme fear and greed will kill your account!

**Fear** and **greed** are those emotions that run in the stock market. They are the same emotions that run in our day to day life. We love this – we hate that...

Fear and greed have a few things in common with each other. First, **they are self-focused rather than having concern for others.** They are also **based on external factors about the future.**

When you have fear and greed at an extreme level, **you will make decisions irrationally as they cloud your judgment.**

Not to mention, since fear and greed are based on external factors, these are all things you cannot directly control and turn off. However, **you can control fear and greed indirectly by reducing your position sizes & taking profits into strength.**

**Your entries, cash, and stops are the only things that you can control in the market.**

You cannot control the movement of the stock price!

**Fear is your response to a threat, whereas greed is your response to opportunity.**

When fear kicks in on the stock market, you can respond in a few ways...

You can do nothing and allow your stock to keep heading lower, and you can hedge, or get out! If you are too fearful, you will do nothing and incur major losses, or you will get out too early.

If you are too greedy, you will load up on a position too big for your experience or hold on to a stock for longer than you should. This will eventually lead to fear as the stock starts its pullback cycle.

These emotions (fear and greed) will whip you around. You will constantly trade based on your emotions and not based on logic and reasoning...

**That's a dangerous place to be with your investments!**

# Rule #16

# Teach yourself patience – know when to sit in cash

Teaching yourself patience is probably one of the most difficult things that I had to learn.

I was quite patient in other areas of my life (at least from my perspective), but when it came to money and the stock market I was still jumping in and out of trades faster than I should have.

**Patience is one of the things that will transform your trading around full circle.**

One of the biggest problems that many novice traders have is not trading the favorable setups that <u>work for them</u>. They trade anything and everything in sight and on any given day, all because they "**feel**" **like they have to trade**. I call this hyper trading and hyper investing.

**Hyper trading and hyper investing will kill your account!**

When you compare hyper trading and investing to a druggie who is looking for their next drug fix – it is not much different.

Both a druggie and hyper trader are constantly looking for something that is not healthy for them. They will do anything to try to get it and make **stupid** decisions to fulfill their cravings.

**Stop being a stock trading drug addict!**

If you are constantly chasing, thinking you "**have to**" trade, forcing a trade, and you are not investing based on your predefined rules, system, and strategy – **then stop! Don't trade and don't invest in stocks!**

Learning to be patient for the right setups, allowing those stocks to set up in your favor, and trading when the conditions are favorable for your trading and investing style is the time to put on trades and be active.

If you are trading in unfavorable conditions – that's like swimming in the middle of an ocean in shark-infested waters at night during a lightning storm without a boat.

Be patient. **Learn to wait until the conditions are set up in YOUR favor. Otherwise, it is going to be a painful road ahead.**

# Rule #17

## Stay away from earnings, events, & big announcements

*"Put all your money into this one stock. Get it while it's hot! Earnings are right around the corner, and it is going to explode to the moon! You are going to make a fortune and become a millionaire!"*

Does the statement above sound something that is in your best interest? **Definitely not!**

**Earnings are major news catalysts that can move the stock in a big** way to the upside or the downside depending on how the company is performing and its outlook. However, you never know when the earnings are going to be good or bad and how it will move the stock.

Even if you can predict earnings to some degree, there are times where **I have seen great earnings, but that stock sells off the next day.** This can happen because the stock may be overextended, the future outlook is poor, overseas problems, or some other reason.

When I was a young and a naive trader – I would constantly trade earnings...

Thinking my stock will beat their earnings... after all, it's \_\_\_\_\_ (company name) and because of \_\_\_\_\_ (put your reason here). **Most of the time things didn't work out. It caused me more stress and frustration.**

**Now I never trade earnings.**

I can avoid earnings all together if I trade the indexes. On the other hand, if I am trading stock, I typically get out before the earnings and get back in later if the earnings are good and the stock reacts positively. Of course, I may miss out on pop, but it also saves me from major drops and huge account losses!

You may think you know better. You may have faith in a company, but **when you experience a massive loss in your account due to earnings, you are going to change your mindset.**

I would say **the only time to hold through earnings is if you have an exceptionally long term outlook in that stock.** If you plan to hold that stock for multiple years into the future, it has proved itself to you from the past, and it is a stable company – **in that case, I may say go for it and hold through earnings.**

Otherwise, if you are trading and investing more actively – get out before the news events and earnings.

**You don't need the headache, stress, and frustration.**

# Rule #18

# Remember the markets return to the mean

Stocks move up, move down, and they move sideways... But in the end, they come back to the mean or the average price that they should be.

Remember that stocks and **the markets move like a rubber band. The more that you stretch it to one direction, the more it will snap back in the other direction.**

This is why stocks that have explosive runs to the upside eventually pull back or have a sideways consolidation move. This sideways move or pull back averages those prices back to the "normal" and "healthy" state.

The same happens when a stock starts a major selloff. **Once a stock starts a major selloff, eventually it will have a significant bounce.** This is where many novice investors get sucked into the hype and eventually lose money.

**When a stock bounces after the first initial selloff, it is trying to average out its price.** The rubber band was too far stretched to the downside. As a result, **the stock pops higher to balance out the trend.**

You might be wondering what happens on these counter-trends and reversals?

**Simple – the winners are taking profits.**

If your stock went to the upside, then you have people selling some shares and the stock pulls back. If your stock was selling off heavily and you see it popping, you have shorts taking profits. Also, other factors start to kick in as well such as value buyers start stepping in and buying a small position.

However, overall stocks come back to the mean.

**You cannot have an explosive move in any one direction in a small period without a reversal in the other direction.**

This is natures law – **things eventually balance out.**

**Expect and embrace pullbacks and retracements as they create new chart patterns.** New chart patterns and pullbacks create fantastic trading and investing opportunities.

# Rule #19

## Technicals will typically trump fundamentals

One of the things I always tell my coaching students is that **"technicals typically trump fundamentals."** Remember this phrase, especially when the market starts rolling over.

Now there is one caveat that goes along with this rule...

In general, stocks that have great fundamentals typically have great charts. The inverse is true. Stocks that typically have great charts... have great fundamentals.

However, **when the technicals break down, and people want to get out – fundamentals do not apply!**

**This happens because a high degree of emotions overpowers our human logic.** This is our natural programming. **When chaos, fear, and emotions kick into high gear, your rational decision making goes out the window.**

When that emotional selling kicks in, it is like trying to get 20,000 people out of a 50 story building during a fire crisis. **The elevator and doors are never big enough!**

It is for this reason I put more emphasis on technical data than fundamental data. Now, of course, I review the fundamentals from time to time, but most of the time if the chart looks good – the fundamentals are typically good.

**In a few of my accounts, I do not trade based on fundamental data at all!** Why is that or how is this possible?

Simple... I trade the indexes like the SPX (SPY), RUT (IWM), or QQQ which I mentioned previously.

**You don't have to do any fundamental analysis when you trade the indexes.**

In the end, fundamental data works in conjunction with the technical data.

However, when the markets start panicking and selling off due to emotional reasons – that elevator door is never big enough, and fundamentals do not apply.

**This is why the technical data will trump fundamental data.**

# Rule #20

# Remember that there is more to life than money

One of the most important rules to remember, in my opinion, is that there is more to life than money.

I know you might be thinking that this only applies to your big-picture lifestyle – and that is true, but it also applies to your success in the markets.

Everything in this world works together.

The world is made up of energy, and it all goes full-circle.

This is one of the reasons that I always stress that **you need to do what you love. Contribute to other people, and live life abundantly.**

We, humans, are social creatures and when you achieve the levels of success that you want – **what's next for you?**

Say you want to make $50,000 a year, $100,000 a year, $500,000 a year, or $200 million – all that money in the world isn't going to connect you with other humans, it won't buy you humility, kindness, and happiness.

Money can make your life easier in the sense that you can do more things with it.

You can travel with peace of mind.

You can hire someone to cook and clean for you to save you time so that you can spend that time with your kids – but **simply having money won't make you happier, kinder, humble, or generous.**

If you are a jerk when you have $50,000, you will be an even bigger jerk when you have $10 million. If you are a kind person without money, you will be even more kind with money.

**Money only exaggerates the type of person that you are because it is a tool in your life. Use it to help you build the life that you want and desire.**

# Final Thank You & Resources

Thanks for reading, studying, and learning from this book. Continue to learn and practice your trading. It takes time to develop a skill, and it doesn't happen overnight. Be patient, be persistent, and you will get what you want. Here are a few website resources I have that you can check out.

- https://tradersfly.com: Free video lessons and training material on stock trading
- https://members.tradersfly.com: Our membership website where you can see some of our premium services
- https://rise2learn.com: List of all the courses and classes that I have created.
- https://backstageincome.com: Learn about building a profitable online business.
- https://mylittlenestegg.com: Website that focuses on personal finance and practical money matters.
- https://sashaevdakov.com: My personal website. See all my training for business, stock trading, and personal finance.

If you have any questions, comments, or suggestions for future courses or training material, feel free to contact me through one of my websites above.

Thanks again,

Sasha

Sasha Evdakov

# More Books by Sasha Evdakov

## Stock Trading Books

- **100 Stock Trading Tips** - The Mindsets You Must Know to Be a Profitable Trader!
- **Start Trading Stocks**: A Beginners Guide to Trading & Investing in the Stock Market
- **245 Money Making Stock Chart Setups (Vol #1)** - Profiting from Swing Trading
- **245 Money Making Stock Chart Setups (Vol #2)** - Profiting from Short Trading
- **245 Money Making Stock Chart Setups (Vol #3)** - Profiting from Penny Stocks

## Business / Other Books

- **Business LaunchPad**: Explosive Business Creation and Growth Strategies!
- **How to Start a Profitable Blog Business**: Creating & Setting Up Your Blog Website
- **Marketing Your Blog Business**: Increase Your Website Traffic, Build Your Email List & Sell More Products

Made in the USA
Columbia, SC
05 January 2021